MW00465848

# DANGERS OF THE MIND
## *30-Day Affirmation Challenge*
### *The Ultimate Guide To Setting Up Your Month*
### *For Peace And Prosperity*

Library of Congress Control Number: 2017904676
International Standard Book Number: 9781543156119
The material contained in this book is provided for inspirational purposes only. Neither the publisher nor the author is responsible for any possible consequences from any person reading or following the advice offered in this book.

Editing: WORDD Enterprises
Graphic Design: Rich Rocket Media

**www.dangersofthemind.com**
**www.twitter.com/@Dangerofthemind**
**www.instagram.com/Dangersofthemind**
**www.facebook.com/Dangersofthemind**

DANGERS OF THE MIND

# 30Day
## AFFIRMATION CHALLENGE

THE ULTIMATE GUIDE TO SETTING UP YOUR MONTH
FOR PEACE AND PROSPERITY

*Kristen Hopkins*

# TABLE OF CONTENTS

# *Introduction*

*O*n life's journey, you will encounter situations that may sometimes discredit your walk, or even cause you to stumble and fall. This happens when you are unaware of the secrets that will help to unfold your true potential, as you aim to fulfill your destiny. You may be reading this book and don't have a clue as to what your purpose is on this earth. But that's ok! You are in the right company.

As a visionary, I am a firm believer, that speaking daily affirmations into the atmosphere, yields phenomenal results. This is what drives me to continue to push through my journey from day to day. While writing this book, there were many moments where I became very discouraged and wanted to give up. But as I started to speak positive affirmations regarding its completion, I was able to achieve my goal. Your mouth is powerful and you have the ability to speak your way into failure or success. The choice is yours! What you say can determine how your day begins and subsequently, how it ends.

This 30 day affirmation challenge is designed to help you eliminate the DOM's (Dangers of the Mind) that could potentially prohibit you from walking in your fullest potential. This is why I encourage you to read my first book. "Dangers of the Mind." prior to beginning this challenge. This book was written and published in an effort to reveal some of the henderances that plague the mind. Therefore, having the full package will equip you further with what you need as you travel on the course of this journey, called LIFE.

Each morning you will see a quote from me, or someone whose wisdom has impacted my journey. Over the course of the next month, you will be provided with the insight on key areas, along with these morning, mid day, and night affirmations that will affect positive changes in your days. You will also be provided with questions that will create an avenue for daily introspection to your current battles of the mind. Challenges are designed to stretch you beyond where you are, and propel you progressively into where you need to be. Although this is a mental challenge, and can get difficult at times, don't cheat yourself out the change that you have been waiting for all this time. Rather keep pressing, and be a part of the change, beginning with the words that you say each day. Are you ready for the challenge?

It's time to commit!

# THE DECLARATION

I _____, vow to do this
30 Day Affirmation Challenge, to better my life
and my every day experiences.

I commit to believing in the affirmations that I
will be speaking into the atmosphere. I will
declare them with confidence, power and
authority. I will not only affect my life, but the
lives of those around me as well. I will remain
consistent in speaking my affirmations every
day and mediate on them at night.
I acknowledge the task that I am embarking
upon, and am ready to experience tangible
results, through the mental shift that will take
place in my life.

# DAY 1

## Forgiveness & Freedom

"Forgive in your mind and your heart will reap the benefits."
*- Kristen Hopkins*

One of the greatest forces that can keep you imprisoned in your life is un-forgiveness. The way that you can get yourself free from the states of immobility and stagnation, is by going through the process that leads you into true forgiveness. Bitterness is a by-product of un-forgiveness, which hinders your growth, alters your destiny, and stops you from entering into the place of prosperity and freedom in your life. It is time to take a leap over the hurdle of un-forgiveness, by repeating the following affirmations.

### Morning
I choose to let go and forgive myself for past mistakes, so that I can freely walk into my future.

### Afternoon
I will allow myself to forgive everyone who has ever hurt me, and I will accept forgiveness from others who I have hurt.

### Night
Tonight as I meditate on forgiveness, I choose to live in freedom and wholeness.

# Inner Reflections

Who do you need to forgive? What hurts do you
need to let go of so you could be free?

_____

_____

_____

_____

_____

_____

_____

_____

_____

_____

_____

_____

_____

_____

# DAY 2

## Power & Influence

"Know your POWER so that your INFLUENCE can live up to it"
- *Kristen Hopkins*

In order to have the right influence, you must recognize and understand who you are, and the power that you possess within. Knowing your personal power can and will determine the influences that come to and from you. This power will guide you into having the right influences in your life.
Turn on your personal power and maneuver through the influences around you, by speaking these affirmations.

### Morning
Today, I will be mindful of the kind of influence that I have on those around me.

### Afternoon
I choose to let the positive influences of those around me impact my life for the better.

### Night
I will continue my journey, knowing who I am on this earth. I am powerful, and I walk with authority.

# Inner Reflections

In what ways can you maximize your personal
Power and Influence?

_____

_____

_____

_____

_____

_____

_____

_____

_____

_____

_____

_____

_____

_____

_____

# DAY 3
## Love & Life

"Love knowing that your life depends on it."

*- Kristen Hopkins*

When there is an absence of love in your life, hurt, pain
and regret are all inevitable. These can cause you to go
through life without living. Choosing to remain buried in
the misery of hurt and pain, can cause the essence of life to
be snuffed out of your very existence. To embrace love,
is to open the portals of productivity and purpose in your
life, which causes you to LIVE AGAIN. Let these affirmations
jump start the flow of love in your life!

### Morning
Today I permit love to overtake my life, and erase the past
hurts that have invaded my heart.

### Afternoon
Today I choose to show love to everyone I encounter
in any little way that I can.

### Night
I will think about the people I care about,
and how can I love them more.

# Inner Reflections

What changes can you make in your life in order
to be more loving?

_____

_____

_____

_____

_____

_____

_____

_____

_____

_____

_____

_____

_____

_____

_____

# DAY 4

## Dedication & Direction

"When you have a clear direction, your dedication should never fail."

*- Kristen Hopkins*

If a life moving in the right direction is a car, then dedication and perserverance make up the fuel. On your journey through life, you will come up against some odds that could keep your life in a place of neutral, and "out of gear" - simply going nowhere. This is when you have to make a conscious decision to stay in gear, and keep moving forward by remaining dedicated and committed to the cause. Begin by using these affirmations to get you moving in the right direction.

### Morning
Today I will perservere,
even when the going gets tough.

### Afternoon
Today, I employ dedication and consistency as
the power to push my life in the right direction.

### Night
Anything worth having is worth fighting and waiting for.

# Inner Reflections

What steps can you take to be more dedicated to moving in the right direction?

_____

_____

_____

_____

_____

_____

_____

_____

_____

_____

_____

_____

_____

_____

_____

_____

# DAY 5

## Atmosphere & Achievement

"Before all else fails, recreate your atmosphere."

*- Kristen Hopkins*

As the main character in the performance of life, it is very important to ensure the stage is set in a way, that can foster the success you desire. Being in control of your atmosphere, and who or what is allowed in it, is what you need to maintain the possibilities, of having your desired outcome in life Begin to recreate your atmosphere as you state the following affirmations.

### Morning
Today I will allow my atmosphere to be made new so that I can walk in my purpose.

### Afternoon
I will make the right choices that will cause my atmosphere to be conducive for positive growth.

### Night
I will commit to achieving greatness, by creating the right atmosphere on a daily basis.

# Inner Reflections

What changes do you need to make to your
atmosphere in order to be successful in life?

_____

_____

_____

_____

_____

_____

_____

_____

_____

_____

_____

_____

_____

_____

_____

# DAY 6

## Brokenness & Bitterness

"If you are dealt the cards of brokeness and bitterness you must remove them from your hand before playing the game."

*- Kristen Hopkins*

If you ever find yourself in a state of brokeness, you must beware of the toxin of bitterness that has a tendency to accompany hurt. By keeping a focus on the negative hand that you have been dealt, it can breathe the deadly poison of bitterness into your life, which can in turn hinder your progress and keep you from fulfilling your purpose. Get rid of bitterness by saying and believing the following affirmations.

### Morning
I will not allow my brokenness to hinder my progress today.

### Afternoon
I will not allow others around me to infuse bitterness into my life.

### Night
Even when I am broken, I will find positive ways to function in my situation.

# Inner Reflections

What is the source of the bitterness in your life?

_____

_____

_____

_____

_____

_____

_____

_____

_____

_____

_____

_____

_____

_____

# DAY 7

## Fear & False Evidence

"Everything you want is on the other side of FEAR."

*- Jack Canfield*

Through the lens of FEAR, things have a way of appearing a lot bigger than they really are. It clouds your perception of your circumstances, which presents hurdles rather than hope. As a result, you spend your entire life rehearsing the excuses of why you CAN'T, rather than believing in the fact that you actually CAN. Fear will always be summed up to "False Evidence Appearing Real". Therefore, it is time to end the rehearsal of fears, and begin practicing the truths, of the possibilities that are ahead of you. As the first in conquering and moving pass your fears, repeat these affirmations.

### Morning
Today I will make a commitment to face my fears,
so that I can conquer them.

### Afternoon
I will no longer remain stagnant because of F.E.A.R.

### Night
I will rest in what I believe about my success
rather than my fear of failing.

# Inner Reflections

What fear do you need to overcome in your life?

_____

_____

_____

_____

_____

_____

_____

_____

_____

_____

_____

_____

_____

_____

_____

# DAY 8

## Perception & Preparation

"Preparation is ready for opportunity.
Perception is ready for a compliment."

*- Sharon Hopkins Wilson*

The actual thoughts of another person are unseen, but they
are often reflected in the way people treat you, or what they
say about you. But this is only others perceptions of you. Too
often, what people think of you, differs from the truth.
Knowing who you are, and preparing your thoughts daily
against what others think, are critical. It is imperative that you
intentionally choose not to confirm to these perceptions.
Furthermore, it is equally important not to allow your mind to
drift into creating perceptions of others, so that the reality
of who they really are, is not clouded. Let us affirm some things
that will guide us on a daily basis.

### Morning
Today I will not let others perceptions of me dictate
the reality of who I really am.

### Afternoon
I am mentally prepared to manage my thoughts
about myself and others.

### Night
I will rest knowing the truth about who I am,
and let it dictate my reality.

# Inner Reflections

What perceptions have you formulated that require a re-evaluation?

_____

_____

_____

_____

_____

_____

_____

_____

_____

_____

_____

_____

_____

_____

_____

# DAY 9

## Complacency & Contentment

"There is a house, and complacency and contentment live there. Burn it down immediately."

-Kristen Hopkins

Unused potential, could be the result of a false sense of satisfaction, that is usually masked by feelings of contentment. Could this be the excuse, for not allowing yourself to be stretched into a place, where you feel a passion for more, and you convince yourself that you are content with where you are, and what you have, it is a detriment to your life's purpose. Begin to ignite the passion for purpose in your life through these affirmations.

### Morning
I will acknowledge the presence of complacency in each area of my life, and determine to change it one step at a time.

### Afternoon
I will encourage others to live above their own complacencies

### Night
I am aware of the comfort zones and complacencies in my life, therefore I will rise above them, to reach my highest potentials.

# Inner Reflections

What steps can you take to eliminate areas of complacency in your life?

_____

_____

_____

_____

_____

_____

_____

_____

_____

_____

_____

_____

_____

_____

_____

_____

# DAY 10

## Insecurity & Confidence

"Nothing holds you back more than your own insecurities."

*- Susan Gale*

When you employ your insecurities as the basis of self-perception, it could become the root of the false opinions, that you have of yourself. It could also cause you to assume others opinion of you. This crippling force, could have a direct effect on the kind of confidence that you need to be able to thrust your way forward, on the path that leads to your destiny. Without this confidence, you will remain stuck in the grip of your own insecurities.

### Morning
Today, I will walk in confidence,
and not dwell on my insecurites

### Afternoon
I will not allow my mind to think that others are
judging me, based on my own insecurities.

### Night
I will rest knowing that by being aware of my
insecurities, I can walk in greater confidence each day.

# Inner Reflections

Identify the insecurites in your life. How have they affected your ability to progress in life?

_____

_____

_____

_____

_____

_____

_____

_____

_____

_____

_____

_____

_____

_____

# DAY 11

"A sharper discernment could be used to pinpoint your distractions."

*- Kristen Hopkins*

Distractions sometimes come disguised as the good in your life, and you will never be able to identify them, if you do not work on sharpening your level of discernment. This is an internal set of eyes that gives way to insight, which allows you to see beyond what is really there. When you make a commitment, to truly rid yourself of the distractios in your life, regardless of who or what they are, you will be more equipped to walk away from them. These affirmations will lead into a life that is free of distractions.

### Morning
Today, I will identify and eliminate the distractions in my life.

### Afternoon
I will only allow people with positive energy.
to be a part of my life.

### Night
I will continue to stay focused on fulfilling my
purpose, as I effectively manage any
distractions in my life.

# INNER REFLECTIONS

*What can you do to heighten your level of discernment, in order to identify and eliminate distractions?*

_____

_____

_____

_____

_____

_____

_____

_____

_____

_____

_____

_____

_____

_____

## PRIDE & EGO

"When Ego irons Pride's wrinkles, pride becomes arrogant."

*- Kristen Hopkins*

The thoughts, ideas and suggestions, that are powered by your Pride and Ego, has the power to thrust you into making decisions, based on clouded judgements. Your own Ego can become so magnified, that great opportunities could appear too insignificant to take on. As a result, you could miss the opportunity to move forward in the right direction, and end up living a life that is rid of both substance and purpose. Let us take a stab at Pride and put Ego where it belongs, by saying these affirmations.

**Morning**
I will make responsible decisions,
without my ego being involved.

**Afternoon**
I will not let pride influence my ability to identify
good opportunites, when they come my way.

**Night**
I will rest knowing that Pride and Ego will
no longer drive my life.

# INNER REFLECTIONS

How have your pride and ego hindered your ability to capitalize on opportunities?

_____

_____

_____

_____

_____

_____

_____

_____

_____

_____

_____

_____

_____

_____

## LIVING & SURVIVING

"If you are living you should be growing. If you are not growing check your roots, soil and how you are nourished."

*- Sharon Hopkins Wilson*

One of the greatest challenges in life, is to press pass the place of simply surviving, to actually living. Very often, you might find yourself existing in cycles of defeat and hopelessness, which has somehow defined your very existence. A choice to LIVE is one of the only ways to break that cycle. Only then, would you be able to welcome the rays of hope and possibilities that have been shining around you all along. Living is the ability to rise above defeat, into victories that come as a result of choosing LIFE. These affirmations will guide you into TRUE LIVING.

**Morning**
Today, my steps will take me into the
direction of meaningful living.

**Afternoon**
I understand the LIVING is far greater
than merely surviving.

**Night**
I will rest knowing that my life has meaning.
and that I am destined to LIVE.

# INNER REFLECTIONS

*Describe any changes that you need to make in order to make your life more meaningful.*

_____

_____

_____

_____

_____

_____

_____

_____

_____

_____

_____

_____

_____

_____

_____

## COMPASSION & CONSIDERATION

"Consider Compassion daily."

*- Kristen Hopkins*

A heart that is rid of compassion and consideration, has a tendency to cast inaccurate judgements on situations, as well as on other people. Whenever you take the time to view a situation or individual beyond what is actually seen, you would often realize that what appears to be, isn't what really is. Compassion will cause you to see beyond the misunderstandings that prevent you from having fruitful and meaningful interactions with others. This will enable you to consider any situation, as being purposeful. It is time to activate compassion and consideration in your life with the following affirmations.

**Morning**
I will be considerate before forming an opinion
about a person or situation.

**Afternoon**
I will have compassion towards others,
even when I don't really know them.

**Night**
I wiill rest in knowing that I was considerate
and filled with compassion today.

In what ways can you welcome more compassion and consideration in your life?

_____

_____

_____

_____

_____

_____

_____

_____

_____

_____

_____

_____

_____

_____

_____

_____

## STRATEGY & REPOSITION

"Develop a strategy today that will help you reposition your tomorrow."

*- Kristen Hopkins*

Change is constant for humankind. Goal achievement and success, are indisputably two things that require strategy to attain. Using strategies that are ineffective, negatively impacts the neccessary steps that need to be taken, in order to be a keen focus on the strategies that you use, to ensure that you are postioned correctly, into purpose and correct alignment. Today, let us make some affirmations that will create the right cohesions between effective strategies, and being repositioned correctly.

**Morning**
Today I will create strategies that align
with the direction of success

**Afternoon**
Every step I take will be beneficial to me,
as I walk out of my strategies for success.

**Night**
I will rest knowing that I am one step closer
to repositioning for greatness because I have
percision in strategy.

# INNER REFLECTIONS

*What new strategies can you implement to get you moving in the right direction?*

_____

_____

_____

_____

_____

_____

_____

_____

_____

_____

_____

_____

_____

_____

## HUMILITY & WHOLENESS

*"Humility is the first step to wholeness"*

*- Kristen Hopkins*

Humility is often misinterpreted by the outer appearance of timidity. However, being humble is a mere appreciation and respect for all human life, and the good that every individual has to offer. It is also the ability to accept confidently, what you have to offer. Wholeness comes as a result of embracing all of humanity, by eliminating the friction of envy and greed toward one another, while humility is the hidden force that makes this happen. Today, let us resound humility in what we say, how we act, and what we do, so that we can be whole.

**Morning**
I will bring wholeness to my life by walking in humility.

**Afternoon**
I will see the beauty and blessings in life, as I see everything and everyone as a gift.

**Night**
I will rest well because I am whole through my life of humility.

# INNER REFLECTIONS

*What are some ways that you can practice more humility in your life?*

_____

_____

_____

_____

_____

_____

_____

_____

_____

_____

_____

_____

_____

_____

## PEACE & SERENITY

"Serenity is the fragrance that exudes from a peaceful heart."

*- Stephanie Brewley*

The state of your inner man is reflected in the way that your enviroment is perceived. Although the enviroment is the same, you could perceive it as cold and mean, or very warm and peaceful, depending on which state of mind you choose to live from. Serenity then becomes the oasis that you can abide in, if you have peace. On a beautiful day like today, go ahead and affirm peace, by the words you say.

**Morning**
I am an instrument of Peace and will remain calm in all situations.

**Afternoon**
I will always be in a state of serenity because of my inner Peace.

**Night**
I am powerful because I live in Peace.

# INNER REFLECTIONS

*Where are you lacking peace in your life?*
*What can you do to have more peace today?*

_____

_____

_____

_____

_____

_____

_____

_____

_____

_____

_____

_____

_____

_____

# DAY 18

"Leadership walks a narrow path with Loneliness."

*- Kristen Hopkins*

Greatness is often said to be accompanied with a price, and is associated with much responsibility. The price tags are heavily disguised and masked by fame and power, which is why the cost of being a leader is highly misunderstood. One of the greatest sacrifices and indications of a great leader, is the call to walk alone. Therefore, rather than welcoming the comfort of fitting in, you must choose to resist the fears of loneliness, and LEAD! Speak overcoming affirmations over your life today as you choose to walk the path of leadership.

### Morning
I will walk confidently even though
I am alone because I am called to lead.

### Afternoon
I am strong enough to leave some people
behind so I can fulfill my purpose in leadership.

### Night
I will rest in solitude because I understand that
my mandate in leadership will require loneliness.

# INNER REFLECTIONS

As a leader, who or what do you need to let go
of in order to fulfill your purpose?

_____

_____

_____

_____

_____

_____

_____

_____

_____

_____

_____

_____

_____

_____

## RESOURCEFUL & RESPECTFUL

"When you are Resourceful to others respect will be
your middle name."

*- Kristen Hopkins*

There is a perfect reason why you are not living in this world
by yourself. Everyone was created with a purpose to fulfill,
and has a responsibility to help someone move closer to their
destiny. Today, respect is almost obsolete, and independence
has been overshadowed by selfishness and disregard for
others. However, it is imperative that you take the time to
respect and appreciate every encounter, so that potential
resources will always be available to you. You must also
remember, that all humankind are resources from an
everlasting and infinite source, that needs to work in unison
to make this life complete. This is a beautiful day, and perfect
opportunity to reflect on, and show respect for every resource
you find, while making yourself available to be resourceful
yourself. Take some time to say these affirmations in
appreciation of the resources around you.

### Morning
I will commit to being Resourceful
to as many people as possible.

### Afternoon
I will Respect every Resource that come my way.

### Night
I will be at Peace knowing that I have been Resourceful
and Respectful towards others.

# INNER REFLECTIONS

*In what ways can you be more resourceful and respectful on a daily basis?*

_____

_____

_____

_____

_____

_____

_____

_____

_____

_____

_____

_____

_____

_____

_____

## STAND TALL & STAND STRONG

"The only way can stand tall is when your foundation is solid."

*- Kristen Hopkins*

The position of your mind determines the posture of your life. Are you Standing Tall? Or are you living a life that is hunched over? Are Standing Strong? Or is life constantly weighing you down? If we really take time to realize it, we will see that life is filled with too many reasons to not stand at all. The option to live is inevitable once you are graced with another day. Speaking life affirmations that will assist you in standing tall and stong are critcal to livng a sturdy life. It can also help you to help others, if you are willing to ensure that everyone else around you is thriving as well. How about verbally affirming, to make this happen for you and others?

Morning
No matter what obstacles life throws my way,
I will continue to stand.

Afternoon
I will commit to helping others identify areas of
weakness and fear so that they can stand strong.

Night
I will rest knowing that I am strong, and
can make it through any adversity.

# INNER REFLECTIONS

*What event in your life has affected your ability to stand strong? How can you work towards getting your strength and courage back?*

_____

_____

_____

_____

_____

_____

_____

_____

_____

_____

_____

_____

_____

_____

_____

# Adversity &
# Opposition

"Purpose is hidden in the Midst of Adveristy and Opposition."

*- Phoenicia Warner*

Life is constantly presented with opposing forces. Subsequently, for every rainy day, there are sunny skies. Or for every beautiful rose that you see, there is a thorny stem attached to it. Likewise, in the midst of purpose and greatness, facing adversity and dealing with opposition are both inevitable. As in sports where you never see one team competing against itself, so it is with your purpose and destiny. You have to get through every form of defense in order to score. Here are some affirmations that can help you to overcome the inevitable if you make them a part of your daily living.

### Morning
I will rise to face opposition, because I understand my purpose.

### Afternoon
I will persevere in the midst of opposition and adversity, because I am walking with greatness in me.

### Night
I will conquer every day, because I understand that purpose does not come without pressure.

# Inner Reflections

What steps can you put in place in order to overcome adversity and opposition?

_____
_____
_____
_____
_____
_____
_____
_____
_____
_____
_____
_____
_____
_____
_____

# Desire & Require

"Knowing what you truly desire will require you
to know who you are."

*- Phoenicia Warner*

Similar to wants and needs, life will present you with a choice
between desires, and what is actually required. As a
responsible individual you must be careful to identify the
difference between the two, and where to channel your focus.
Nothing is absolutely wrong with having both. However, the
challenge is to create balance by prioritizing, so that a life of
deficit doesn't become your portion. Mastering the ability to
identify what you require, and setting the precedence. you will
in turn allow you to attain your Desires eventually. Let your
affirmations of desire and require lead you into a life of
ulitmate fulfillment each day.

### Morning
Today. I commit to understanding the difference between
what I Require, and what I Desire in life.

### Afternoon
I live in the understanding that not everything
I Desire for my life is what I Require.

### Night
I am confident beacause I know how to balance
my requirements and my desires.

*Inner Reflections*

How have you mistaken between your desires and what you require to be successful? How has this affected your progress in life?

_____
_____
_____
_____
_____
_____
_____
_____
_____
_____
_____
_____
_____
_____
_____

# Strength
# & Comfort

"Allow your Strength to bring you to a place of Comfort."

*- Geraldine Findley*

The words tough and hardcore, are often affiliated when making references to the word Strength. Let me challenge your philosophy a little bit, by sharing that, people who have Strength often need Comfort. It is in the times when you are challenged to do something outside of what the natural response would be, that Strength is required. Finding Comfort in those times can be difficult, but making a conscious effort to identify positive Comfort sources, and resorting to them, does require Strength. Here are some affirmations that will channel you into this practice.

### Morning
I am a strong person because I am quipped with
the capacity, to act outside of what I feel.

### Afternoon
I will be careful to seek positive sources of Comfort,
even at times when I am feeling Strong.

### Night
I commit to becoming Stronger every day,
knowing thatI find Comfort in spite of my circumstances.

*Inner Reflections*

What positive sources of comfort have you ignored
in an effort to remain strong?

_____

_____

_____

_____

_____

_____

_____

_____

_____

_____

_____

_____

_____

_____

# Networking &
# NETSURFING

"Collaborate with people you can learn from - NETWORKING!
Get lost in poeple you can follow - NETSURFING!"

*- Kristen Hopkins*

The World Wide Web has multiple spheres on influence that
reach a wide range of audiences. In fulfilling your purpose,
you dare to do some introspection. Who or what is keeping
you glued to the screen? And what effect do they have on your
purpose in life? Who do you have in your network?
The answers to these questions will let you know what kinds
of repercussions will come as a result. It is important to
consciously choose to connect with what will move you into
destiny. An accurate balance betwen the influences of social
media and "people connections", will enable you to grow in
purpose successfully. Make this happen intentionally, by
affirming these words.

### Morning
Today I walk in confidence that the right sources
will meet me in my path.

### Afternoon
Today I will not allow technology or social media to
dominate my decision making.

### Night
I will rest knowing that I am capable of balancing the
networking and netsurfing components of my life.

# Inner Reflections

How has the use of the internet prevented you from building a positive network?

_____

_____

_____

_____

_____

_____

_____

_____

_____

_____

_____

_____

_____

_____

_____

_____

# Kindness &
# A Pure Heart

*"When you start looking at people's heart instead of their face, life becomes clear."*

*- Unknown*

Like a cup that is filled to the brim, whatever is in your heart, is what will flow out when life gets shaken up. This is why you should be careful to examine what you let into it. Kindess and gentleness can only flow out of a heart that is pure and filled with love. Similarly, out of a heart of hatred, will only flow negaitve emotions which can lead to unthinkable actions. The world is in need of kindness, and soaring higher altitudes depends on it. However, it will take a pure heart for it to flow out of you. Try these affirmations to help you block out the negative emotions, so that kindness can flow freely.

### Morning
Today, I will commit to being Kind to everyone I meet.

### Afternoon
I will be mindful of negative thoughts and circumstances, and will not let hatred enter my heart.

### Night
I will live in peace, because I walk in Kindness, and my heart is pure.

# Inner Reflections

What practical ways can you add more kindness
and purity into your heart and life?

_____

_____

_____

_____

_____

_____

_____

_____

_____

_____

_____

_____

_____

# Identity & Authenticity

"You were born an original, don't die a photocopy."

*- Dr. Kingsley Fletcher*

The value of any note of currency is lost, when it is replaced by counterfeits. Likewise, if you spend your time living as a counterfeit of someone else, you end up replacing your identity, diminishing your authenticity, and ultimately, losing your value. This world has a place and purpose for everyone, born with a unique set of characteristics and factors that make up who they are. When you choose to leave the gift of who you really are in the wrapper, your place in the world is left unoccupied, and your true identity is left unseen. The truth is, there is only one of you and the world awaits the gift of who you really are. Make a decision to affirm authenticity and value to your world today, by knowing and being you.

### Morning
I will make every effort to be the real me,
so that others will identify with my true self.

### Afternoon
I will embrace who I am, because the uniqueness
I bring to the world, no else can.

### Night
I will rest knowing that by me understanding who I am,
I will no longer settle for less than I deserve.

# Inner Reflections

In what ways have you changed your identity in an effort to fit in? What have you tried to hide about yourself from the people in your circle?

_____

_____

_____

_____

_____

_____

_____

_____

_____

_____

_____

_____

_____

_____

_____

# Purpose & Persistence

"When you know your purpose, the key is to stay persistent."

*- Kristen Hopkins*

Against all the challenges and circumstances that life presents, living according to purpose, will require a steady hand to the plough. The temptation to quit and throw in the towel will always be there, when the going gets tough. But that is when you have to make a conscious decision to keep you to your destiny. Giving up is never an option, when success is weighing in the balance. The more aspiration to follow through with Persistence, will drive you into your Purpose. Let us take some time to practice some "Persistence in Purpose" affirmations.

### Morning
Today I will be Persistent in striving towards my goals, so that I will be one step closer to my dream.

### Afternoon
I will commit to staying focused on what my purpose is, so that I can live each day to work towards fulfilling it.

### Night
I will dream big, so that I can continue to presistently move daily, in the direction of my purpose.

# Inner Reflections

Describe a time when you gave in to temptation to quit. What can you do to get your life back on track with purpose and destiny?

_____

_____

_____

_____

_____

_____

_____

_____

_____

_____

_____

_____

_____

_____

_____

# Self-Worth & Misjudgement

"Don't allow your misjudgment to devalue your self-worth."

*- Kristen Hopkins*

The value that you place on yourself, will determine the kind of vision you will have for your life, and the level of success you will have for your life, and the level of success you will allow yourself to attain. Your decisions will be directed per the price tags that you have attached to yourself as an individual. Subsequently, you cannot expect to be treated as a valueable piece of China from a speciality store, with a flea-market price tag. One of the greatest understandings you can have, is that of your own self-worth and value. Without this understanding, you will be constantly misjudged by others, and yourself. It is time to see yourself as the valueable gem that you really are, rather than accepting any kinds of treatment from others. Take some time today to affirm the right value over your life.

### Morning
I will guard the true value of my life.

### Afternoon
I will commit to dismissing every
degrading thought about myself

### Night
Every day, I will be treated with respect,
because I know who I am.

# Inner Reflections

What thoughts do you have about yourself that are misaligned with who you really are?

_____

_____

_____

_____

_____

_____

_____

_____

_____

_____

_____

_____

_____

_____

# Faithfulness
# & Fruitfulness

"Being faithful is like planting a seed every day with the
expectation that you will reap a fruitful harvest."

*- Kimberly Jackson*

Consistency and faithfulness go hand in hand, and will make
way for positive results in your life. The kinds of seeds that
you sow, always determine the kinds of fruit that you will be
produced. In your garden of life, it is important to be mindful
of the kinds of seeds that you sow. Being faithful in pulling
up weeds of negativity, and nuturing the plants of positive
attitudes that will bring fruitfulness into your life, are
important tasks on your part. In order to change the
undesirable results that you have been seeing in your life, you
must plant different seeds. Let us commit to saying these
affirmations, that will lead us into being faithful and fruitful,
so that we could begin bearing good fruit.

### Morning
I am faithful over every positive practice that
I have committed myself to.

### Afternoon
I will reap the benefits of a successful life,
because I will remain faithful in all good things.

### Night
I understand the importance of speaking positively,
so that I can experience a good life.

# Inner Reflections

*Evaluate your faithfulness, and identify changes that can be made to increase your fruitfulness.*

_____

_____

_____

_____

_____

_____

_____

_____

_____

_____

_____

_____

_____

_____

# Trust
# & Truth

"The naked truth is always better than a best dressed lie."

*- Unknown*

In order to gain Trust, there must be the presence of Truth, which begins in the inner man. This where we commit to being true to ourselves, and to others. In order to go through life successfully, you have to be true to yourself, which ultimately gives way for you to trust others. On the contrary, dishonestly and deciet will eventually have free reign, when Truth is not practiced. Subsequently, the lack of trust could cause you to be short-changed, as you strive to reach your goals successfully. By repearing these affirmations, you will continuously shift your inner and outer atmosphere, to reflect and attract Truth.

### Morning
Today I will be true to myself, so that I may be trustworthy in my performance.

### Afternoon
Today I commit to understanding that I can trust others, because I can trust my true self.

### Night
I will perserve in truthfulness, against the odds.

*Inner Reflections*

In what ways can you be more true to yourself?

_____

_____

_____

_____

_____

_____

_____

_____

_____

_____

_____

_____

_____

_____

_____

_____

# The Reminder

FREE yourself and learn to FORGIVE,
So that you won't just SURVIVE... but LIVE!
STAND TALL and STAND STRONG
no matter what comes along.
Be COMPASSIONATE AND CONSIDERATE,
even when you've been done wrong.
Rid yourself of INSECURITIES and build CONFIDENCE
in who you were born to be.
Always walk with KINDNESS and A PURE HEART.
This guides you in PEACE and SERENITY.
You may have been BROKEN but don't become angry or BITTER.
And remember, you have enough STRENGTH to find COMFORT,
because you are not a Quitter.
ADVERSITY and OPPOSITION will come,
at every stage in this life.
But remain RESOURCEFUL AND RESPECTFUL,
throughout the trials and strife.
Be TRUE to yourself, so that you can TRUST others as well.
Learn to LOVE yourself Back to LIFE,
so you'll have a beautiful story to tell.
Go boldly toward Destiny and use DEDICATION
to push you in the right DIRECTION.
But sharpen your DISCERNMENT,
so that you are not overcome by subtle DISTRACTIONS.
Ensure that your STRATEGIES align well, and in cohesion for REPOSITION.
Don't waiver in being FAITHFUL, and you'll be sure to see your
FRUITFULNESS and Possession.
Be mindful of who you NETWORK with and NET- SURF
for positive plans.
Be PERSISTENT in PURPOSE in every way,
because work and life go hand in hand.
Know your SELF WORTH and don't you MISJUDGE
who you really and truly are.
Don't let PRIDE AND EGO step into your sphere,
or you would not get very far.
It is ok to have a life of CONTENTMENT but not of COMPLACENCY.
And In order to be WHOLE in this precious life,
walk in HUMILITY.
LONELINESS may come sometimes,
but remember the LEADER in YOU.
Don't crumble. Don't break. Stand up to the fight.
Your destiny is surely in view.
Your ACHIEVEMENT in life depends greatly on a
positive ATMOSPHERE.
Knowing your POWER determines your INFLUENCE,
and this can take you anywhere.
PREPARATION of your mind will guard your
PERCEPTIONS into a marvelous light.
Imagine a life based on lies, as you are blinded by sight.
Live a life of Balance knowing what you REQUIRE and DESIRE.
Remember the person that understands the difference,
will get what they need to go HIGHER.
FEAR will render you hopeless; It is FALSE EVIDENCE appearing real.
Walk boldly in your true IDENTITY and AUTHENTICITY,
despite the way that you feel.

Want more affirmations and encouragement for the months to come?
Subscribe to our monthly newsletters by logging onto
www.dangersofthemind.com TODAY!

DANGERS OF THE MIND